ILFRACOMBE
A PICTORIAL RECORI

GLENN K. HORRIDGE

AMMONITE BOOKS
GODALMING

First published 1986
©Glenn K. Horridge 1986

Ammonite Books
58 Coopers Rise
Godalming
Surrey GU7 2NJ

Typeset and printed by Adlard & Son Ltd, Dorking, Surrey

ISBN 1 869866 00 2

ACKNOWLEDGEMENTS

I would like to thank the following for the loan of photographs, information and help so freely given: the Curator, Mrs Joy Slocombe, the Trustees and helpers of Ilfracombe Museum; Mrs Olive Arscott, Jan and Eddie Bennellick, John and Sue Janaway and last, but by no means least, my mother, whose knowledge of her native town has proved invaluable.

INTRODUCTION

The picturesque town of Ilfracombe, nestling in the rugged North Devon countryside, has for centuries welcomed people for relaxation and pleasure. Its mild climate and healthy ocean breezes attract visitors all year round.

In the Domesday Book of 1086, the name Alfreincoma, meaning the wooded valley where Alfred dwells, was first used. Other forms of the original were Hilfrincombe and Ilfradiscombe. By 1249, Ilfracombe had been divided into the Champernowne family and De Tracy family manors. These and other families held the manors up to the beginning of this century.

During the later Norman period, the harbour became particularly important as an embarkation point for Ireland. In 1208, King John assembled a fleet here to make the crossing. Henry III did the same in 1246. Edward III ordered sea ports according to their size to send men and vessels to aid his invasion of France in 1346. Liverpool sent one vessel and five men; Ilfracombe sent six vessels and 96 men. The seaport remained vital and in Elizabeth I's reign nearly 1000 soldiers at a time marched to Ilfracombe for the crossing to the Irish wars.

Apart from its strategic importance, Ilfracombe was also a major centre for merchant shipping. Coasters ranging from 7 to 30 tons crossed the channel to Wales and Ireland with cloth, brass, soap, foodstuffs and cattle. During the English Civil War of the 1640s and 1650s, Ilfracombe suffered greatly. On 20th August 1644, the Royalist Sir Francis Doddington attacked this Parliamentarian stronghold, burning 27 houses but losing many men. This took place around the area now occupied by Brookdale Avenue and Wilder Road, which thereafter became known as Bloody Meadow. Doddington was unsuccessful but three weeks later Ilfracombe's commander surrendered the town to General Goring. Twenty pieces of ordnance and 200 arms were handed over. Ilfracombe with its castle, which was built in Tudor times to protect the harbour against French pirates, was held for the King until 1656 when Cromwell's Colonel Sheffield stormed the town.

The threat from France remained as constant as the cruel sea. Royal Naval vessels and their captured prize ships often docked at Ilfracombe. On 9th October 1796, the 600-ton troop ship *London*, carrying 150 prisoners of war, was wrecked in Rapparee Cove. Thirty prisoners in the hold were drowned but other prisoners, troops, passengers and crew were saved. Tragically, 16 local men were drowned attempting the rescue.

The *Illustrated London News* in 1856 suggested that the *London* was sunk by the wreckers and smugglers common in Ilfracombe. They would tie lanterns to horses' tails and walk them along the cliff to decoy vessels. Smugglers' tunnels did exist from the coast to deep inland such as Sampson's Cave, which surfaced at Chambercombe Farm. Even a revenue cutter named *The Shark* (nicknamed *Coombe Shark*) failed to stamp out smuggling after 1800.

In 1797 upon the approach of French warships, a local woman, Betsy Gammon, gathered others and, beating a drum, she led them over the hillsides with their red petticoats over their shoulders. The idea, apparently successful, was to convince the French that British Redcoats were on the march.

Twenty years earlier Ilfracombe was already known as a good watering place in which to spend at least part of the summer season. J. M. W. Turner was commissioned to paint Ilfracombe views in 1811. The town's increasing popularity was marked by the number of famous visitors. Admiral Nelson stayed at the Britannia Hotel. The writers Charles Kingsley, Daniel Defoe, George Eliot and Beatrix Potter all gained inspiration whilst in the town. Royalty also visited and were no doubt impressed by the Tunnels Beaches cut in 1823 and the steam packet, *Duke of Lancaster*, which regularly called at Ilfracombe from 1822 on its trips between Cork, Swansea and Bristol.

During the 19th century the tourist trade remained seasonal but other trade flourished. In the preceding century over 60 sloops, schooners and smacks were launched from the shipyard on the south side of the harbour. The yard continued to employ men and although the last commercial vessel, the 101-ton *Cloffock*, was launched in 1865, John Pollard built small cutters of which at least two are still afloat as yachts. Nearby, men from Rope Walk supplied the mariners with cordage. Fishing was another major industry with large catches of herring common off Ilfracombe. The Strand contained smoking and salting houses.

Perhaps the town's most impressive building was the Ilfracombe Hotel opened in 1867. The laundry, now the Museum, is the only part of this once famous hotel to have survived. In 1874 the Ilfracombe railway was completed, making the town even more popular as a holiday resort. In 1888 the Victoria Pavilion was erected to commemorate Queen Victoria's Jubilee.

Within local folklore the origin of the First World War is told. Prince Frederick William of Prussia spent a holiday at Ilfracombe in September 1878. Caught throwing stones at bathing machines on Rapparee Beach, he became involved in a fight with the young attendant, Alfred Price. The prince came off worse and promised to return for revenge. It was only natural when war was declared by Kaiser William that this story be celebrated in verse.

This century has seen many changes affecting the town. A large number of public works marked the first decade. In 1901 Alexandra Hall, which was named after Edward VII's queen, was opened. In 1904 a new town water supply was provided, whilst three years later the pier and harbour were purchased by Ilfracombe Council. The pier was in ever-increasing use, especially by pleasure steamers.

Following the First World War, which took the lives of 157 townsfolk, holidaymakers returned in force and the town thrived once more.

The number of hotels increased and the motor car made travelling easier. During the Second World War Ilfracombe became essentially a garrison town. The Royal Army Pay Corps, for example, occupied the Ilfracombe Hotel.

Since the war the town has lost a little of its Victorian splendour. The Ilfracombe Hotel has been demolished, the pier rebuilt and the use of the harbour has declined. The railway was closed on 20th October 1970 and the station sold. In September 1983, the Arcade and Candar Hotel were destroyed by fire and in 1985, the Beacon Castle Hotel was similarly razed to the ground.

However, Ilfracombe remains popular with the thousands of visitors who still find relaxation and entertainment in this attractive area, just as their great-grandparents did 100 years ago.

Glenn K. Horridge
May 1986

To my Mother and Father, without whose help and encouragement
this book would not have been produced.

1. This engraving of the town and harbour in 1774 was dedicated to Sir Bourchier Wrey, lord of the harbour manor. This was the ancient settlement of Ilfracombe before its Victorian and Edwardian expansion. The harbour, with its crenellated wall, is busy with sailing ships of all sizes but there is no promenade pier. The Chapel of St Nicholas built on Lantern Hill in about 1300 was then, as now, a prominent landmark.

2. This painting of harbour and town shows, on the far right, the wrecking of the transport ship *London*, which arrived off Ilfracombe from St Lucia during a storm on 9th October 1796. All attempts to secure the ship to the buoys failed and she drifted on to Rapparee Rocks. Sixteen local men were drowned during the rescue and many black French prisoners trapped in the hold were also lost. A quantity of treasure was spilt into the sea.

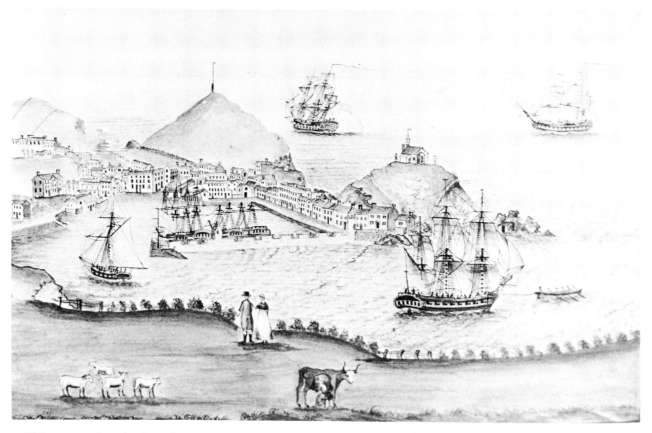

3. This watercolour by Joseph Waters was painted in 1805 at the height of the Napoleonic Wars. Lookouts were posted on Lantern Hill. The British man-of-war in the background to the left appears to be engaging the approaching enemy. The smaller ship in the foreground is being positioned by ship's boat to speedily catch the wind. Frenchmen often ventured up the Bristol Channel to attack shipping.

4. A quieter scene painted in August 1805 from the east side of Hillsborough. The Wrey manorial home can be seen standing in isolation to the far left of the church. Below it a ship is under construction in the shipyard.

5. This view of Ilfracombe from Hillsborough was drawn by George Rowe in 1829. The harbour wall has been built up and imposing Georgian villas dominate the town. By this time steamers had already began to call at Ilfracombe.

6. The town became rapidly built up after the 1820s. The deteriorating condition of the parish church led to the foundations of the church of St Philip and St James being laid in 1851. The church was completed in 1857 and its spire can be seen prominently behind the harbour. This 1874 engraving shows the steps down to Rapparee Cove and the promenade pier, completed in 1873.

7. Ilfracombe from the Torrs in 1872, showing Capstone and Hillsborough in the distance. A line of imposing villas marks further expansion of the town, whilst the neat new tree-lined roads indicate some thought for the future.

8. This 1911 view shows the extent of the Victorian and Edwardian building. Despite the loss of the shipyard, Ilfracombe was compensated by its ever-increasing popularity as a seaside resort.

9. Before the promenade pier was built, the only way over to the north side of Lantern Hill was via steps hewn out of the rocks. The paddle steamer is arriving to pick up passengers from the harbour slipway for the cross-channel trip to Wales.

10. Walking up and down Quayfields, watching the harbour, has always been a popular pastime. The path also gave an excellent view of boats under construction.

11. The shipyard set into the Cove can be seen in this engraving, just above the end of the harbour wall. During construction of a ship, a temporary wall was built to hold back the sea. On completion the wall was removed to allow the ship to float on the next high tide.

The words "SHIP BUILDING AT ILFRACOMBE MAR. 1851. 107." appear on the hull in the photograph.

12. The scale of employment in the shipyard and subsidiary industries was considerable. In this detailed picture the owners' and managers' wives are viewing the hull of one of the larger vessels under construction. The industry probably commenced in the early 17th century and ships up to 100 tons were launched over the next 250 years.

13. The late Victorian fishing fleet was large for the harbour size. Here some vessels and crew are shown in the summer of 1890. Herring were plentiful and salting took place just beyond the buildings shown on the right.

14. This Edwardian photograph of the southern side of the harbour shows now-demolished fishermen's boathouses and cottages.

15. On the north side of the harbour, the numerous hotels did a roaring trade thanks to the steamers which plied the Bristol Channel. Stories are told of inebriated visitors rushing out of the bars at night and crossing the street in an attempt to board their ships. This early 1890s view shows no railings or wall to prevent them from sobering up quickly in the harbour!

16. In 1772, a French prize ship captured by Admiral Rodney in the West Indies went aground on the rocks at the base of Hillsborough. The Admiral's only consolation was, perhaps, this public house and lane which were named after him.

A Bit of Old Ilfracombe.

17. The entrance to Rodney Lane at the bottom of Fore Street about 1890. The right-hand building is the Prince of Wales public house and next to it, the Labour Exchange.

18. This 1885 photograph is of Lifeboat Square, so named because the rowing boat used in pre-RNLI rescues was stored here. The entrance to Fore Street is on the left with the corner of the Ebrington Arms just visible. These mainly one-up one-down cottages have gone and only the railings survive today.

19. A turn of the century view looking down Fore Street towards Hillsborough and the harbour. The police station was situated halfway down on the left, next to the school. The whole street, one of the oldest in Ilfracombe, remains largely unchanged.

20. Near the top of Fore Street was Gardner's Boarding House and Refreshment Rooms. This photograph was taken in 1890 from Somers Crescent, shortly before the property was rebuilt as the Montebello Hotel.

High Street, Ilfracombe.

21. The eastern end of the High Street in 1905. To the left, Fore Street descends to the harbour and, to the right, leading up to Hele and Combe Martin, is Portland Street. Cole's bedding and furniture shop occupied the central position.

22. Joseph Parrett's store about 1897. Wines and spirits at reasonable prices were among the main specialities of this store. It seems that stealing letters from window signs is nothing new! Above the shop was the Masonic Hall and the stone emblem is still visible today.

23. Looking east along the High Street towards Cole's and the harbour, the start of the remaining split level or bank can be seen. On the far left is the Ilfracombe depot for the famous Honiton lace and next door, Furse's grocery shop.

24. Detail of 15 High Street, W. W. Furse's shop about 1895. The Town Hall was situated above and beside it and, leading from the arches, ran Market Street.

25. Two children watch the traffic from the bank opposite 19 and 20 High Street, looking west, in about 1905. The 'taxi' rank was conveniently located in what is now the middle of the road. A fountain and trough for horses stood just below the children. This part of the bank was removed in 1934.

26. Saying goodbye to the troops. Many of the crowd stood on the bank to get a better view of the local territorials as they marched to their embarkation point for France on 8th August 1914. Many of these soldiers did not return.

27. A busy part of the High Street. No. 96 was the main booking office for Sam Colwill's famous coach-and-four excursions. The next building with the porch is the Queens Hotel. The Post Office, Braund's, Northfield Road and Myatt's were opposite.

28. Sam Colwill drove visitors around Ilfracombe and district. He is the gentleman with the beard standing in the foreground. His son Tom is driving. No. 97 High Street was the office of the London and South Western Railway.

29. Braund, whose corner shop is prominent on the left, was well known in and around Ilfracombe as a tea dealer and grocer. This rare and much battered photograph shows the building which still deals in refreshments, as it is now the long-established Boni's Cafe.

30. On the opposite corner to Braund's was Myatt's establishment, with the entrance to Northfield Road on the right. This photograph of 1899 shows a huge variety of goods arranged to catch the eye of the visitor. Miss A. Slocombe's Scientific Dressmaking Rooms were located through the entrance to the right of the shop.

31. Further down the High Street, the Congregational Church stood next to Green Lane in which the Queens Hotel stables were situated. This photograph was taken about 1891.

32. The dining room of the Queens Hotel. The napkins arranged in a floral pattern indicate the ladies' places. A small library of books was available to patrons courtesy of the 'Commercial Travellers Christian Association'.

33. A sample of a High Street shop interior about 1890. This is Catford's photograph and art gallery in typical Victorian congestion.

34. Montpelier Terrace about 1905. These imposing houses were built in the early 19th century and were taken by various well-to-do families for all or part of the summer season.

35. The Old Cottage, now the Thatched Inn, was built in the early 1800s and today still retains much of its character. Its original name was Larkstone Cottage and here lived Albert Price, the boy who fought the Kaiser.

ILFRACOMBE ST. BRANNOCKS RD. OPPOSITE THE PARK.

PHOTO PHILLIPS

36. These fine houses are typical of the building which took place in the west of the town. Admiral Nelson sent Lt. Edward Down to Ilfracombe to help control smuggling. He later became a rear admiral and his descendants occupied a house in this Victorian row.

37. Another example of Victorian architecture, this time Gilbert Grove, photographed in 1908.

38. Tuckey the chimney sweep was a well-known local figure, as he pushed his cart loaded with brushes around the town. He is pictured here in front of the Cliffe Hydro Hotel, Hillsborough Road. The hotel was originally built as a private residence for the Bourchier family and was named Quayfield House.

39. Ilfracombe's parish church, in 1864 during the 51-year incumbency of John Mill Chanter, friend of the Clovelly vicar and his novelist son, Charles Kingsley. The church dates from the early Norman period although a Saxon timber church is believed to have stood on the site. Local legend says that three maiden ladies gave this land and an endowment to build the church, dedicated to St. Mary Magdalene and the Holy Trinity.

40. The Lych Gate is well known for its intricate stone carvings. The major core of the church was extended to its present size in 1321, at a cost of £40. Various further alterations have been made over the centuries. The variety of interesting shapes and wording on the tombstones reflects a similar variety of commemorative tablets inside.

41. This view of the parish church and Church Road in about 1906 gives an indication of its impressive position on the west side of the town.

42. To commemorate the opening of the railway to Ilfracombe in 1874, celebration arches were erected along the High Street and at other significant points, such as outside the Ilfracombe Hotel. This magnificent arch of flowers and greenery was outside the Town Hall.

43. Further down the High Street from the Town Hall, this very welcoming arch celebrated the same event as the previous photograph. On 20th July 1874, bands led a procession to announce the opening of the railway. They passed under all the main arches, each of which bore a different motto such as 'Queen of the West' and 'May the Rails of the New Line Never Rust'.

44. Ilfracombe railway station and town from Cairn Top. Two steam engines were needed to pull a train into the station as the incline or 'bank' south of the town was the second steepest in the country, two miles of 1 in 36.

45. Station Road in 1910. The area around the station was gradually built up and many of the houses became guest houses. They were popular with visitors who had not previously booked and, of course, were in an excellent position to attract them.

46. This is a view from the railway station looking down Score Valley, with Cairn Top to the right. The tide of building gradually extended along the valleys and up the southern slopes.

47. Slade Valley in 1905. As yet little building had taken place here and the railway line skirted the hamlet.

48. Apart from the magnificent houses, the Torrs were and still are noted for breathtaking zigzag walks along the cliff-side paths. On a sunny day the three mile stroll over to Lee is still most invigorating. Here the refreshment pavilion commands an unparalleled view of town and channel.

ILFRACOMBE - THE TORRS WALKS.

49. Visitors had to pay a one penny toll for the privilege of enjoying the Torrs walks, which are now free. These walks were constructed on the seaward side of the seven peaked hills, known locally as the Seven Sisters, to the west of the town.

50. The tunnels to the beaches were cut by Welsh miners in 1823. This engraving of 1838 shows the Tunnels entrance and the Doric style baths, built in 1836. Underneath the main ground floor of the Bath House was a labyrinth of small enclosures where hot or cold sea water baths could be taken for health or hygiene.

51. Thomas Copp's coach 'Alert' stands in front of the Baths House in 1896. The building had changed little in 60 years but the view now included to the right, Runnymede Villa, which was built in about 1845. Here Charles Kingsley, George Eliot and other notable writers took residence at various times.

Rock & Co London No 1342.

30 Aug 1860

52. The path in this engraving of 1860 led through the last passage to the Ladies Bathing Cove. The crenellated walls were in keeping with the irregular coastline and rocks.

53. This is the Ladies Bathing Cove from the sea in about 1835, with the crenellated wall on the right and the Capstone on the left. According to local legend, a bugler sat between the ladies' and gentlemen's pools. If a man dared to creep round the rocks to spy on the ladies, the bugler would blow an alarm call and the man was promptly arrested!

54. Although only one pool remains today, the ladies' pool, it is still very popular. However, in 1905 mixed bathing was allowed for the first time and, as this photograph of 1912 shows, was obviously enjoyed by all.

55. The people in the foreground of this 1890 photograph are sitting on the lawn of the Montebello Hotel. They are awaiting the start of the 'White Coons' show, a minstrel entertainment which was very popular with the visitors. In the background a group of musicians are holding a concert on Wildersmouth Beach.

56. By resting on the rocks or taking a promenade, holidaymakers could enjoy the sea breezes but not, in the case of the ladies, the sun. The 'fair' sex carried parasols to prevent the acquisition of an unfashionable suntan. In the corner of the beach is Preachers Rock, an ideal and still used 'pulpit' from which to preach the gospel.

57. Although carefully posed, this early photograph portrays the popularity of walking around the Capstone. The walk was cut during 1842 and 1843, at the height of the 'Hungry Forties', and was opened on 14th September 1843. The aim was to give work to unemployed men and their wage was a loaf of bread and a shilling a day. The total cost of £220 was raised by public subscription.

The Promenade, Town, Ilfracombe.

58. A view of the town from Capstone walk in the 1900s with the West Bandstand at the bottom. Its ornate ironwork was testimony to Victorian craftsmanship and in the season, the band played there morning and evening. In the distance is Somers Crescent on the left, leading up to Fore Street. The road to the right led into a shopping arcade and through to the High Street.

Ilfracombe. Windy corner during storm.

59. A favourite occupation of both young and old is still, as it was in 1910, walking around Windy Corner. Even a mild breeze seemed strong and few could walk it in a gale. The walk on a windy day is now even more difficult as the protecting wall is lower. The hand-rail was a late Victorian addition.

60. This 1864 engraving shows the popularity of Capstone Parade. Taking the air while watching ships sailing in the Bristol Channel was a favourite pastime with visitors.

61. Cheyne Beach, Lantern Hill and Hillsborough are clearly visible beyond Capstone Parade. The lack of a protecting wall must have added to the excitement.

62. To get a better view, the zigzag paths could be climbed and were obviously very popular, as this Edwardian picture shows. The harbour lies to the right of Lantern Hill. For the more energetic, a climb up Hillsborough was possible.

63. This rare 1903 picture shows the Electric Telegraph Company's signal-staff and the coastguard semaphore apparatus on the summit of Capstone. In the 18th and 19th centuries coastal communications relied on this method of signalling, which could also be read by shipping. The small building on the left, built into the cliff, was the swimming baths belonging to the Ilfracombe Hotel.

64. To get down to the rocks from the Capstone Parade for adventure or fishing, steps known as 'The Forty Steps' were cut in the later Victorian period. They were frequently recut after severe winters. This picture was taken in 1901.

65. For the lazy or infirm visitor to Ilfracombe a donkey cart or a donkey ride was a popular means of touring the sights. This photograph dates from the early 1890s but donkey transport had been available to visitors for at least 100 years before that.

66. One of the byelaws of the pleasure grounds stated that these small vehicles should have 'one ass and not more than one passenger'. Although similar to the other carriage, the means of propulsion is here rather different – a dutiful son or son-in-law perhaps?

THE ROPERY MEADOW, ILFRACOMBE

67. A complete circuit of Capstone Parade brought you back to Ropery Meadow and the seafront shops. The local Board of Health bought the meadow in 1882 for £2203, for use as a recreation ground. The directors of the Ilfracombe Hotel had planned, in the previous decade, to build a winter garden, aquarium, skating rink and concert hall on the site.

68. The beautiful Ilfracombe Hotel was opened in May 1867. Centrally located with excellent views, the hotel was for some time the most palatial in North Devon. There were 210 rooms including a ladies' dining room. Some bedrooms had connecting bathrooms and a few were especially designed for invalids. Hot and cold running water was piped throughout the building.

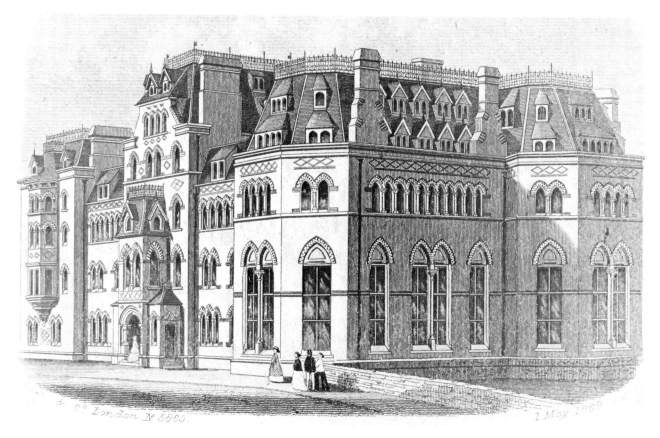

69. This engraving was commissioned for the Ilfracombe Hotel's first anniversary in 1868. In 1871 a west wing was built, adding a further 40 rooms. Double rooms cost between four and six shillings per night, with servants bedrooms at one shilling and sixpence. A tremendous choice of food could be had and the day started with the possibility of four different breakfasts. The laundry, now Ilfracombe Museum, is the only remaining building.

70. The iron and glass Victoria Pavilion was opened in 1888. Apart from commemorating Queen Victoria's Golden Jubilee, the aim was to provide a shelter for visitors 'to enjoy a promenade in inclement weather, besides providing a winter garden to assist in the restoration of the invalid to robust health'.

71. A concert platform and seating were placed in the centre of the Victoria Pavilion. The aquaria were a constant tourist attraction, as were the varieties of plants, whilst the whole structure was lit by gas. Locals gave it the nickname of the 'Cucumber Frame'.

72. Most of the buildings shown in this 1892 photograph survive today. St James' Place is on the left, as is the church of St Philip and St James. The 'handsome and commodious' Wesleyan Chapel and adjoining school houses in the foreground have since disappeared. This area was originally very sandy and the sea came in further than today. Boats were tied up in the vicinity of the church, which is itself built on sand.

73. On the night of 15th–16th December 1910 a combination of tide and wind brought a tidal wave sweeping over Wildersmouth Beach, flooding Ropery Meadow. Here, looking from the beach towards the Collingwood Hotel, an idea of the devastation can be gained.

GREAT GALE. ILFRACOMBE, DEC 16, 1910. 29

74. Here is another view on 16th December 1910 of the damage caused by the tidal wave. Boarded up windows are visible and the cost of repairs ran into thousands of pounds. However, the local children found it an exciting play area.

75. The original Cole's furnishing establishment was the source of 'The Great Fire at Ilfracombe'. The alarm was raised at 12.40 on the morning of 29th July 1896. Within four hours, 35 business premises and houses had been burnt to the ground and many others damaged. The absence of any wind helped to prevent an even greater disaster. At its height the conflagration was visible across the Bristol Channel in Wales.

76. The full extent of the devastation was evident next morning, when nothing remained of Cole's shop. The flames had darted across Fore Street and set the Arcade alight. The Arcade acted like a funnel and fire poured down, destroying the 14 shops as well as houses. The fire also spread up and across Portland Street.

77. Inside the Arcade before the fire where Twiss and Sons lost eight shops and two houses. However, the hard work and feats of bravery by fire brigade, police, coastguards and others saved the town. By a miracle, no one was killed.

78. This is the ruins of the Arcade looking towards the High Street. In September 1983 a similarly destructive fire here destroyed the entire rebuilt Arcade and the Candar Hotel. Instead of the horse-drawn fire engines, this time 22 fire tenders attended from all over North Devon. In sad contrast to the fire of 1896, one person died in this recent fire.

79. The houses in any part of old Ilfracombe are of great variety, as is the photographer's punctuation! The sign on the wall, which still exists, was made from single blue tiles with white lettering. Such tiles were produced in Barnstaple and were a speciality of the area.

80. The Golden Lion was one of the oldest buildings in Ilfracombe. It was demolished between 1893 and 1895 when the Quay was widened. The advertisements on the side wall make interesting reading and 'Rizine' foods, particularly puddings and custards were very appetising.

81. Mr R. Martin, Ilfracombe's Town Crier in the early 1900s, was one of the very few in England on horseback. He had been a soldier and took great pride in his appearance.

82. Mr Tom Davey was an equally familiar sight in the town. He was one of a family of 13 children, brought up by their parents in the Chapel of St Nicholas on Lantern Hill.

83. This hotel was built in Wilder Road in 1884 and is now known as the Berkeley Hotel. An advertisement in the mid-1890s claimed that it had perfect sanitary arrangements, hot and cold baths and spacious ladies' drawing rooms.

84. The Granville Hotel dates from 1891 and was named after a leading 19th century temperance figure. It contained 40 bedrooms as well as a billiards room. 'Sociable, Select and Comfortable. A bona-fide Temperance House, Noted for Delicious Coffee' said an 1895 advertisement. To the right, the Cardiff pilot boat heads towards the harbour.

RUNNACLEAVE HOTEL, ILFRACOMBE.

OFFICIALLY APPOINTED—ROYAL AUTOMOBILE CLUB.

Telephone
No. 36.

MRS. CHOWN,
Manageress.

"THERE is no pleasanter or cheaper place of cure (to indulge in a puff honest and true) than ILFRACOMBE, with its quiet nature, and its quiet luxury, its rock fairyland and its sea walks, its downs & combes, its kind people, and —if possible—its still kinder climate."

Charles Kingsley.

85. Completed in the summer of 1891, this hotel had 120 rooms plus a large recreation hall for theatricals and dances. There was also a photographic darkroom, indoor skating rink and games room. The hotel also boasted its own omnibus to meet every train and its own pleasure yacht for the use of visitors.

86. The Imperial Hotel was well advertised as a private establishment which specialised in personal attention. It is still as recognisable today as in this turn of the century picture. The bank in the foreground has also survived.

THE COTTAE HOSPITAL ILFRACOMBE
BATTEN PHOTO

87. In 1864 Mrs Anne Tyrell provided two beds for sick people in her cottage, Such was the demand that, on 27th August 1868, the foundations of the Tyrell Cottage Hospital were laid. By 1900, 25 beds were available for visitors and locals alike. Guided tours of the wards and theatre took place on three afternoons a week.

I am coming home from ILFRACOMBE.

88. A touch of Edwardian humour but still true today.

89. The paddle steamer *Eclair* seen at anchor, protected by Lantern Hill and the tip of rock known as Warphouse Point. This photograph dates from before 1872, when the building of the promenade pier was commenced. The Golden Lion is visible to the left and the lifeboat station to the right. The Chapel of St Nicholas on Lantern Hill was built about 1300 and probably doubled as a lighthouse from that time.

90. After the construction of the promenade pier, several paddle steamers at a time could tie up side by side. Passengers could then cross from ship to ship to disembark and re-embark. Left to right, the vessels are the tug, *Privateer* and the paddle steamers, *Brighton, Ravenswood, Scotia, Westward Ho!* and *Lorna Doone.*

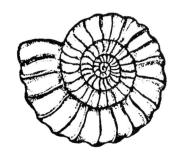

For full details of our publications please write to:

Ammonite Books
58 Coopers Rise
Godalming
Surrey GU7 2NJ